Looking Back

ANZA and GARNER VALLEY

Margaret Wellman Jaenke

Library of Congress Card Number:
200 2092193

ISBN 0-9719661-3-3

Printed in the U.S.A. by
Morris Publishing
3212 East Highway 30
Kearney, NE 68847

*Dedicated to the memory of
two homesteaders,
my parents,*

Elma Grace Hall
and
James F. Wellman

Illustrations

CONTENTS

A Note to the Reader

Much of the mountain history and many of the old stories have been lost forever. Very little has been written about the early settlers and homesteaders and their way of life in Anza and Garner Valley. Except for the two very good books by Lester Reed, not much has been written by anyone who actually lived in the hills and knew what life was like in the time of dirt roads and no electricity.

My hope is that this little book will help those not having that experience to better understand what it was like for the early settlers who came in their wagons, worked, and hoped for a better life.

For additional copies of this book contact:
Margaret Wellman Jaenke
31901 Box Elder #8
Mountain Center, CA 92561

Chapter

1

A Place of Change

Looking back at the history of Garner Valley and Anza constant change can be seen in more than one way. Place names have changed, the way of life has changed, and even the people living there have changed.

Over the years Garner Valley has been known, at different times, as Hemet Valley, Thomas Valley, Pine Meadows, and Kenworthy. The valley, now called Anza, has gone by the names of Cahuilla, Cahuilla Plains, Hamilton Plains, Babtista, and Baptiste. This change in place names and sometimes post office names is a cause for confusion in telling about the history of the area.

Change in the way of life in the mountains has been even more striking, especially in the last two hundred and fifty years. First it was a place inhabited only by the hunting and gathering people native to the area. In the middle 1800s the mountains became a region of farmers and cattle ranchers. That same area of the mountain region is now home to thousands of people from many different cultures and from many different parts of the world. Few now make a living as farmers or cattle ranchers, even those whose families have lived here for many

1

generations. Most workers are employed off the hill and take advantage of paved roads to commute to work elsewhere. All use and enjoy the electricity and the numerous other services found in any modern society.

The changes that have modified the way of life the most, have taken place in the last fifty years, the time after electricity, irrigated farming, and paved roads were introduced to the area. Until the middle 1950s the people in Garner Valley, Anza, and the surrounding areas, except for Idyllwild, lived much like the people in the Midwest had lived in the 1800s.

With no electricity, reading or doing anything after dark required a lantern or a kerosene lamp. Homes were warmed only by wood burning stoves or fireplaces. There was a telephone at Lake Hemet, but until the late thirties Anza had none. The first, and for many years, lone telephone in Anza, for "emergency use only," was the phone that had been installed in the Devaney's store by the Forest Service in the late thirties.

The main occupations of the early pioneers were the raising of cattle and dry farming. Schools were makeshift affairs in barns or homes, or at best a schoolhouse with only one room and one teacher for all eight grades. Mail delivery at the hill country post offices was a sometime thing. If the dirt roads were in poor condition mail didn't always arrive, even on the two or three days a week that were scheduled for mail service. After a winter storm or a heavy summer rain, the roads were often so muddy that it was impossible to get in or out of the valley or down the mountain for days, or even weeks at a time. At that time the only sure way to travel up or down the mountain was on foot or by horseback.

Local grocery stores usually carried only the basic commodities. San Jacinto in the earliest times, and later Hemet, were the nearest places to do any serious shopping. Before automobiles came into use and there were better roads a trip down the hill by wagon to shop could take at least three days. Highway 74 had been paved by the 1930s but Cahuilla Road, the main highway through Anza, wasn't paved until much later in the 1950s. There was no road to the desert, only Indian trails and old cattle trails.

Life in the hills changed rapidly in the nineteen fifties when the Anza Electric Cooperative began supplying electricity to the entire area for the first time. Another big change was the paving of Cahuilla Road, now State Highway 371. Even more changes were brought to the hills when telephones were finally being installed in homes by late 1959.

With all this modernization other people soon found the hill country to be a more attractive place to live. Those working were still able to live here and continue to work by commuting off the hill over the improved roads. Retired people came looking for retirement homes.

Before too many years had passed further modernization took place. A bank and an improved modern grocery store were built on the site where Clark and Nell Devaney's old general store had served the community for so long.

Soon there were dentists, doctors, and veterinarians to take care of the health needs of the residents and their animals. The school was modernized, and in more recent years it has become a K-12 school. High school students are no longer compelled to go down the hill to further their education.

The changes made in the Anza and Garner Valleys over the last fifty years are changes that were undreamed of for anyone living here during the early part of the twentieth century.

"If I were you, Jim, I'd stick to a horse!"
(Jim Wellman and his first car.)

Chapter

2

First Mountain Residents

For hundreds of years, some say even thousands of years, the San Jacinto Mountains have been home for the Cahuilla Indians. People from the Cahuilla Reservation in Anza and the Santa Rosa Reservation to the east were all strong and intelligent people who had learned to live and flourish in an environment that was not always the easiest to even survive in.

The weather was often harsh and it could be extremely cold and windy in wintertime. Rain might be scarce or altogether nonexistent. Adequate rain was essential for the plants and the animals that these hunting and gathering people were dependant upon.

Their food gathering area, in addition to what is now reservation, took in all the surrounding hillsides and valleys, including Garner Valley, the higher mountains around Idyllwild, and down into the lower regions around Palm Canyon and Pinyon Flats. Any food surplus was stored for later use or for trade with others.

The Mountain Cahuilla people had developed a way of life that allowed them to make the most of what they did have. Through cooperation with the Desert Cahuilla and Pass

5

Cahuilla, as well as with other native people, they had worked out a system where in time of need or drought the different groups were often able to help each other by trading food.

There are many signs of these people living here in times past. Bedrock mortars, rock shelters, pottery shards, and other artifacts scattered throughout the hills and valleys can still be seen. This is especially so where there was once an abundance of oak or pine trees and a source of water. In early times the plowing of most any field was likely to uncover a buried arrowhead, matate, or mano. Rocks and caves often have examples of Indian art known as pictographs and petroglyphs.

The Cahuilla basket makers are well known for their artistry in the making of beautiful baskets, many decorated with intricate designs depicting Indian life and their surroundings. The sturdy and well-made baskets are often watertight and were used for cooking vessels. Cahuilla made baskets are displayed in museums throughout the world. Those with the likeness of a rattlesnake woven right into the basket are especially well known.

Cahuilla people have long been a vital part of the mountain community life. They were able and valued employees on the early ranches and farms. The Costo, Lubo, Cassero, Tortes, Hamilton, and Guanche families, as well as many other families, were all productive and valued citizens in the early days. Among those still living in the mountain area are many respected citizens taking an active and creative part in all aspects of life in the high country.

A bedrock mortar used by the local Cahuilla
Indians to grind seeds and acorns.

The Cahuilla Indian cemetery with Cahuilla
Mountain in the background, about 1940

7

Chapter

3

Juan Bautista De Anza

In 1774 and 1775, Juan Bautista De Anza and his fellow explorers journeyed from Mexico to Monterey in northern California. According to diaries kept by these travelers, they passed directly through the southern part of what is now known as Anza Valley.

After riding up through Coyote Canyon they camped at the site of the Fred Clark Ranch, now known as the Cary Ranch, in Terwilliger Valley. Anza called the place San Carlos Pass. The explorers' diaries mention the beautiful lake at the southern end of the valley. That lake, on the northern edge of the Cahuilla Reservation, is now usually just a low dry spot, but in former years, in times of more rain it was actually a lake. Even in the middle nineteen hundreds there was enough water to attract geese and other waterfowl.

Juan Bautista De Anza's first horseback trek through the valley in 1774 was one of exploration. He was looking for an easier and more direct route from Mexico to San Francisco. At that time there were no roads, stores, motels, or other conveniences that the travelers of today require. Most everything needed by the travelers was carried with them on horses and mules. After passing through the Anza area they traveled by way of Bautista Canyon on down to the San Jacinto Valley and San Gabriel Valley, and weeks later finally reaching the San Francisco area.

The second Anza expedition, in 1775, was a more complicated endeavor. That trek would move more than 250 people, their livestock, and their household goods to start new homes in Northern California. The group was made up mostly of young families, with a large percentage of the travelers being children under the age of twelve.

Anza's journeys are commemorated with three bronze plaques, one at the Fred Clark ranch in Terwilliger Valley and another down in Coyote Canyon. A third smaller plaque, a trail marker with the date only, is on the large boulder outside the old Hamilton School, now called the Little Red Schoolhouse. The large bronze plaque at the Clark Ranch describes both journeys. The plaque in Coyote Canyon marks the spot, where it is claimed the first white child was born in California during the second journey.

Recently two exhibits about the journeys of Juan Bautista De Anza have been placed outside the library at Hamilton High School.

Juan Bautista De Anza and others in his group kept very detailed journals. These old records give excellent descriptions of the entire journey along the route that was followed from Mexico to northern California. Anyone interested in the journeys of Juan Bautista De Anza should look at these old diaries written by the men who were actually involved in the expeditions.

Juan Bautista De Anza Plaque
In Terwilliger

The plaque reads, *"On March 16, 1774 Juan, Bautista De Anza, Indian fighter, explorer, and colonizer, led through this pass (named by him San Carlos) the first white explorers to cross the mountains into California. On December 27, 1775, on a second expedition, into California, Anza led through this pass the party of Spaniards from Sonora who became the founders of San Francisco," Tablet placed by Historic Landmarks Committee. Native Sons of the Golden West. 1924*

Chapter

4

FIRST SETTLERS

Before the middle eighteen hundreds the only permanent inhabitants in the Anza Valley were the Cahuilla Indians. Miners, trappers, and hunters came into the area, but were just as apt to move on and not settle down to make homes.

One of these early miners who came, discovered gold in the hills above Garner Valley on the eastern side of the valley, and then moved on, was Jesus Contreras. He was the grandfather of Antone and John Contreras, both early homesteaders in the Anza Valley.

Those people who did come and stay long enough to establish permanent homes were usually not miners, but were cattle ranchers looking for good pasture and grazing land for their livestock.

In the late 1860s the David and Frances Reed Parks family settled south of Cahuilla Mountain in an area directly to the west of the Cahuilla Indian Reservation. That entire region soon became known as Parks Valley, a name it was known by until recent years. In the 1970s when Parks Valley was subdivided the property was renamed Lake Riverside Estates, the name it is now known by.

The Parks family had arrived in California from Texas in 1867. They came over the

11

Southern Emigrant Trail in wagons pulled by teams of oxen. The family was looking for a place to raise cattle. When they found the grassy meadows just to the west of the reservation it seemed to them to be just the right place for their ranch.

For nearly a hundred years the family farmed and raised cattle there and at times ran cattle down into Coyote Canyon. One of the canyons in that area became known as Parks Canyon, for Isaac Parks who had as a young man camped there while tending the family's cattle.

At least five graves belonging to this homestead family have survived the building of many homes and roads, as well as the other changes that have taken place over the years. Two headstones, those of the mother, Frances, and one son, Jesse, are located on the island that was once just a knoll in the middle of the cow pasture. The graves of another son, Joe and his son Robert, are both on the western side of the valley near the site of Joe's old home. David A. Parks, the homesteader, is buried near the site of the original Parks home.

The quiet grass-covered valley with gently rolling hills is no longer recognizable as the Parks ranch. Many homes surround a man-made lake and the busy state highway cuts through the property. There is even an airstrip where cattle once roamed.

Arriving in the hill country at about the same time as the Parks family was the Quitman Reed family. The two families had come together from Texas. The Reed family, also searching

12

for good grazing land, settled on the western side of Cahuilla Mountain in what is known as Reed Valley. Many descendents of the large Reed family continue to inhabit the surrounding area. The late Lester Reed, author of several books on the hill country was a member of this family.

Others arriving in the 1860s at approximately the same time as the Parks and Reed families and also looking for grazing land for their livestock, were the Will and Shasta Tripp families. These two men, Will and Shasta, were sons of Samuel Tripp, a man who for many years was a prominent judge in the San Jacinto Valley.

The younger Tripps homesteaded west of Anza Valley on the eastern slopes of Cahuilla Mountain in what soon came to be known as Tripp Flats, a name the area still retains. Another place named for this family is above Garner Valley at the end of Morris Ranch Road. Now it is most often known as Trail's End but on many maps it is still listed as Tripp Meadows, a name earned because of the Tripp family's use of that area as a garden spot.

With many mouths to feed, Shasta and Will Tripp took advantage of the rich black soil and the abundance of water found there to grow much of the food needed for their large families. Old timers used to tell how the teenaged boys in the Tripp family were sent there each spring to grow vegetables, especially potatoes.

At that time the area was sometimes even called the Potato Farm or Potato Ranch by the locals, but the name Tripp Meadows was the name shown on maps for many years. Violet Tripp Woods and Irene Tripp Medley, descendents of this pioneer family continue to live in the Tripp Flat area.

M. G. Wheeler, the U.S. Deputy Surveyor, noted that in 1876 there were only two settlers in the Cahuilla Plains, one a Mr. Vines and the other James Hamilton, the owner of a thriving ranch on the eastern side of the Cahuilla Plains.

All trace of the mysterious Mr. Vines seems to have disappeared, but there are many records of James Hamilton, a highly respected citizen and rancher. Federal census records of 1870 show the Hamilton family as near neighbors of the Parks family just west of Anza in the Temecula District, of San Diego County.

Still another record placing the Hamilton family in the valley in the 1870s is a report in the California State Mining Bureau Bulletin printed in 1905. The bulletin notes that Henry Hamilton, the teenage son of James Hamilton, had discovered the first colored gem tourmaline in the state of California in June of 1872. Signs of the once profitable Columbia mine, as it was called, can still be seen along the Thomas Mountain road at about the 5,000 foot level.

James Hamilton, a man of mixed racial background, was born in Ohio around 1821. He came to San Bernardino, California in the middle 1800s with a Mormon wagon train. After spending some time in San Bernardino he moved to San Diego where he was a hotelkeeper.

An interest in the cattle business drew him to the mountains northeast of San Diego. There he was soon raising cattle and had started a family. The mother of his children was an Indian lady from the mountains around

14

Julian. Because of a difference of opinion about property rights the family left the San Diego mountain area and moved to property near Temecula. Again they were forced to move when that land turned out to be a part of the Vail Ranch.

The next and final move for James Hamilton, by this time a widower with four children, was to what was then called the Cahuilla Valley or Cahuilla Plains. There he filed on homestead land at the northeastern side of the valley. His home was situated between Hamilton Creek and Thomas Mountain. In time Hamilton cattle ranged over the entire eastern part of the Cahuilla Plains, up around Hog Lake on the side of Thomas Mountain, down into Coyote Canyon, and over into Garner Valley.

The original James Hamilton home is gone but a white adobe house now stands on the exact spot where the Hamilton house had been built over one hundred years ago. (In the late 1930s the Jim and Elma Wellman family built the house that is now seen there.) In order for a part of the Hamilton family to take care of their cattle on both sides of Thomas Mountain a second home was built in Garner Valley. That house was on the northeast corner of what is now the intersection of Toolbox Springs Road and Devil's Ladder Road.

Water for the Hamilton home in Anza came from a spring in the draw above the house supplying sufficient water for the household and the cattle. Besides raising cattle, the Hamiltons had a garden, fruit trees, bees, rabbits, and chickens to provide them with food. At that time the nearest shopping was in San Jacinto.

James Hamilton and his family were all very well thought of and highly respected throughout the mountains and the surrounding area. By the late eighteen hundreds many people were referring to the eastern part of the valley as Hamilton Plains. Seventeen years after James Hamilton's death a name was needed for the new school district. The community chose the name Hamilton in his memory, a name the district kept until 1964 when the Hamilton School District was taken over by the Hemet Unified School District.

Almost thirty years after James Hamilton's death, the people in the valley continued to want to honor his memory. This time it was in naming the post office. They chose the name Hamilton, but there was already a Hamilton City in the northern part of the state so the name Hamilton could not be used. Anza was finally settled on for the new post office name in 1926.

Mary, the oldest of the four Hamilton children spent her entire adult life in Anza keeping house for her father and brothers. She was a talented young woman noted for her fine needlework. Some of her handwork was shown in the Smithsonian Institute and at Stanford University. Mary was also well known for her skill as a seamstress and maker of beautiful quilts.

Living in a time and place where friends and relatives were far apart, and there were no telephones with which to keep in touch, Mary spent a great deal of time writing to friends. Hundreds of letters, written by friends and family in reply to Mary's letters, have survived for over one hundred years. These letters provide a clear picture of life in the hill country in the 1880s and 1890s.

Joseph, the second of James Hamilton's children, was also raised on the family's cattle ranch in Anza and continued in the cattle business all his life. In later years he spent most of his time at the Hamilton home in Garner Valley.

Joe Hamilton had two families. The first family consisted of one son, Augustine and his mother Rosadia Powette. Later Joe's son, Augustine and his wife Caroline Apapas, were the parents of two sons, Frank and Jimmy. Many descendents of this family continue to live in the mountain region.

Joe's second family consisted of Lincoln Joseph (Punk), Agnes, Lucy, and Frank Montgomery (Gummy) Hamilton, and their mother Clara Arnaiz. This second marriage also included Clara's two children from her first marriage, Mary and James Wellman. According to Mary and Jim, Joe Hamilton was always a loving and kind father treating all his children and stepchildren in the same fair way.

Henry was the third child in the James Hamilton family and spent his entire life in Anza and Garner Valley in the cattle business. He filed and proved up on 160 acres of homestead land on the south side of Highway 371 about where Ciro's restaurant stands. Henry's acreage was one of the few in the valley to have a surplus of water. His generosity in sharing that water with those less fortunate was known throughout the valley. In earlier days the property surrounding Henry's well was a lush green meadow with

17

many meadowlarks and other birds. The house had disappeared by the late 1920s but the old wooden barn remained for many years. Henry Hamilton never married and lived as a bachelor until his death in 1933.

"You have lost a good brother at the hands of a villain," were the words a friend wrote in a letter to Mary Hamilton in April of 1895 when her brother Frank, the youngest of James Hamilton's children, was shot and killed. Frank had been on duty as a constable for Riverside County and had stopped at a restaurant in Bowers, the old section of San Jacinto, where he checked in his guns.

Before that day was over Frank and a bystander, Al Larson, were both shot and fatally wounded by Charlie Marshall, a man of questionable character. Feelings against Marshall ran high in both Riverside and San Diego Counties.

There was even talk of lynching Marshall. The opinion was expressed by another letter writer and seemed to be the feelings of many county residents. *"I hope the man who did the deed will be hung. He is trying very hard to get out, but if he does get out I hope the Cahuilla boys will get him and lynch him."*

Over the years several versions of that day's events have come to light, each a little more lurid than the last. Some versions make it sound like there had been an authentic wild west shootout between the good guys and the bad guys. Other accounts describe a barroom brawl. Court records prove otherwise.

Testimonies of the witnesses confirm

18

that it was actually murder of both Hamilton and Al Larson on the part of Marshall. There was in fact an exchange of gunfire between Marshall and Hamilton, but it was established in court, without a doubt, that Charlie Marshall was the aggressor and had fired the first shot without warning. That first shot fatally wounded Al Larson, with the bullet going through Larson's body and then injuring Hamilton. Those acquainted with Hamilton and his ability with a gun, all agreed that if he had seen Marshall's gun in time the outcome would have been entirely different.

On the surface it seems that Marshall did the double killing without any reason at all, but old-timers felt that in the line of duty as an officer of the law, Frank Hamilton had learned more than the criminal element of the county wanted him to know. For that reason, Marshall, described by many as an undesirable character, wanted Hamilton out of the way and murdered him in cold blood.

From the testimony of eyewitnesses to the killing it was brought out in court that Marshall had earlier made racial slurs and derogatory remarks to and about Hamilton. At that time both men were unarmed, but Marshall had said that if he had a gun he would shoot Hamilton.

Throughout that encounter Hamilton, known for his good sense and fine manners, was polite and respectful and kept saying that he wanted no trouble. To quote another old letter, *"Ever body that knew Frank spoke well of him, even those that didn't know him spoke well of him."*

From all accounts of the eyewitnesses it

19

was felt that by the time that Hamilton and Marshall had gone their separate ways, the earlier misunderstanding had been peacefully settled. That turned out to be a false assumption. After leaving the building Marshall had tried to borrow a gun from one man and was turned down. He tried again and succeeded in getting the loan of a gun from Ed Nelson, who went home, got the gun and gave it to Marshall. Nelson failed to ask Marshall what he intended to do with the gun. What Marshall did was to go looking for Hamilton.

By that time Hamilton had retrieved his own guns and was ready to leave for another part of San Jacinto. Marshall found Frank leaning against a building talking to his friend, Al Larson. Without any warning Marshall opened fire, fatally wounding Larson who was standing in the way.

That first bullet, shot by Marshall, went through Larson's body and also hit Hamilton's right arm, hampering his ability to defend himself. Several more shots were fired, at least one by Hamilton, a shot that hit Marshall in the abdomen causing a nonfatal wound. The coroner and the attending doctor testified that Frank Hamilton had received six gunshot wounds throughout his body, including the fatal shot to his abdomen.

After two trials, one in May of 1895 and another in July of 1896, Charlie Marshall spent several more years in the penitentiary for the killing of Larson and Hamilton. Later he was paroled to the Garner ranch in the San Bernardino Mountains where he lived out the rest of his life as a ranch hand.

Soon after the Parks, Reed, Tripp, and Hamilton families arrived in the hills other settlers began to come into the Anza valley. The Terwilliger family was one of those first families. Jacob and Almira Terwilliger, natives of New York, and their children, Albert, Mary Jane, Amelia, and Annie first came to California by covered wagon around 1875.

The family lived for some time on the north side of the San Jacinto Mountains at a place called Hall City, the starting point for the lumber wagons going into the mountains around Idyllwild to haul timber down the mountain. In about 1883 the family came to the hill country and settled at the south end of the valley in what was soon being called Terwilliger Valley.

Unlike most early settlers the Terwilliger family did not come to raise cattle. Their interest was more toward farming. About ten years later, when the new county of Riverside was formed from parts of San Diego and San Bernardino Counties, Jacob Terwilliger became the first justice of the peace in the Cahuilla Valley.

By around 1891 the Clark brothers, Fred and Frank had also come to the valley. The brother's aim was to raise cattle. For many years they both ran their cattle down into Coyote Canyon and lower to places like Clark Dry Lake, Clark Well, and Clark Valley, all named for these two early ranchers.

Frank's home was in a little valley called Durazno Valley on the other side of the Cahuilla Indian Reservation to the south of Anza. Frank and his wife, Annie Terwilliger raised their children, Vermal (Bud or Bub) and Lola at their ranch in Durazno Valley. Frank was a cattleman all his life and lived on his ranch in Durazno Valley until his death in 1937. Son Vermal lived most of his adult life in San Jacinto. Lola and her husband Howard Bailey continued to live on the ranch and to run cattle until their deaths.

Fred Clark bought land in Terwilliger Valley from a man by the name of Pesqual Powett. It was known as La Puerta ranch. The large bronze plaque commemorating the journeys of Juan Bautista De Anza through the Anza Valley is on that property situated just south of Coyote Canyon Road. The property was for many years known as the Fred Clark ranch. Fred had built himself a small adobe building where he continued to live as a bachelor for the remainder of his life. A pile of disintegrating adobe brick, which can still be seen south of Coyote Canyon Road, is all that is left of the house where Fred lived until his death in 1938. Two of the adobe bricks from Fred's house have been saved. One is on exhibit in the Hamilton High School library and the other is in the "Little Red School House."

In later years Fred's interest turned more to horses rather than to cattle. In the late thirties, shortly before his death Fred Clark sold his ranch to Art and Violet Cary.

In Hemet Valley, now called Garner Valley, on the other side of Thomas Mountain, or "over the hill," as the early mountain inhabitants would say, other cattlemen were arriving at about the same time as the Parks, Reed, and Tripp cattle ranchers were moving into the lower elevations around the Anza area. Many of those settlers in Garner Valley also came to take advantage of the good grazing land that was found there.

In the mid 1860s Charley and Genoveva Bardico Thomas, former residents of the Temecula area, chose the northern end of the Hemet Valley for their ranch and then stocked it with prize cattle and fine racehorses. They too, had come looking for good pastureland. There are several accounts of how Charley Thomas came into possession of the many acres of land that made up the ranch. There are stories of bets and gambling, and others of deals made with the Indians.

Soon the northern end of the valley and the mountain to the southwest of their ranch became known as Thomas Valley and Thomas Mountain. Some old-timers said that the mountain was named for Charley Thomas. Other stories dispute that and say that the mountain was really named for his wife, Genoveva, because she was the one at home raising their twelve children and running the ranch. Charley was seldom home. He was usually away with one of their older sons running their prize racehorses

In 1907 the Thomas property was sold to R. F. Garner. That end of the valley then became known as Garner Valley. Before coming to the San Jacinto Mountains the Garner family had been in business in San Bernardino and for many years had been cattle ranchers in the San Bernardino Mountains. It was only after the southern end of the valley was subdivided in the 1970s, the part that had been known as Kenworthy, that that area also became known as Garner Valley. Members of the Garner family still

23

live on a part of the property that was the original Thomas Ranch.

Coming soon after the Thomas family was Frank Wellman. He at first worked as a ranch hand for Thomas family and as a teamster for the Scherman lumbers mills around Idyllwild. Before long he, too, had his own cattle business with cattle grazing in Thomas Valley, around Idyllwild and on the side of San Jacinto Mountain. Place names there reminding one of this early day cattleman are Wellman Cienega, and Wellman Divide.

Frank Wellman came to California from Iowa with his parents as a two-year-old child and was raised in San Bernardino. Frank later married Clara, the oldest daughter of Manuel and Dolores Arnaiz, early homesteaders in the Garner Valley area. Two children were born of this marriage, Mary Margaret and James (Jim) Wellman.

The Arnaiz family arrived in 1891 in Hemet Valley also looking for grazing. Manuel Arnaiz was born in San Francisco, the son of a sea captain, Eugenio Arnaiz and his wife, Teresa De Monroy Arnaiz. At a young age Manuel left home and made his way south while working on different cattle ranches. Arriving in southern California he met and married Dolores Garduna, the daughter of Jose Aducto and Marta Valenzuela Garduna of Agua Mansa, Colton, California.

Manuel and Dolores Arnaiz had lived in Yucaipa for several years where four of their children Eugene, Clara, Daisy and Fanny were born. Hearing about the excellent grazing

24

land, which could be had for homesteading in the San Jacinto Mountains, they moved the family and their large herd of cattle to the grassy meadows southeast of the Thomas Ranch.

Four more children, Daniel, Edward, Ernest, and Henry were born to the Arnaiz family after moving to the mountains. One child was born in Valle Vista; the others were all born at the family homestead in Garner Valley.

Most of the early settlers came to raise cattle but soon dry farming became an important part in the life of the pioneers. Dry farming is the raising of crops without the benefit of irrigation. The only moisture that the crop would receive was rain. If the rain didn't come at the right time and in the right amount there would be no crop. The hay and grain produced made winter feed for the livestock. If they had a very good year there might be a surplus to sell.

Hunting played a major role in the life of hill residents. Most of the early settlers did at least some hunting. Being a successful hunter and bagging a deer or some rabbits could make the difference between eating well and not eating well. Many discovered that a young cottontail rabbit made a very tasty addition to a meal.

The trapping of coyotes, bobcats, skunks, and other animals, and the sale of their furs were ways of earning money in an area that did not have many opportunities to earn cash. That cash might enable a struggling family to survive and continue living in the hill country. Many young boys earned their first money by hunting and trapping. Ambitious youngsters sometimes set a trap line that was checked as they went to and from school.

Chapter

5

Lake Hemet Dam

When Lake Hemet Dam was completed in 1895 it was considered, by many to be one of the wonders of the world. At a height of over 122 feet it was not only the highest masonry dam in the world, but many of the obstacles that at the time seemed impossible to overcome, had been surmounted.

To begin with the only road up the mountain was the Crawford toll road through Idyllwild. There was not a direct route up the mountain to Garner Valley, the site proposed for the future dam. William F. Whittier and Edward L. Mayberry, the two businessmen and land developers were dreaming of putting together an adequate water system for irrigation and domestic use in the San Jacinto Valley, especially for the new town of Hemet.

These two men took care of the road problem by hiring men using picks, shovels, and horse drawn Fresno scrapers. They soon completed a shorter, less steep route, than that of the old Crawford toll road. The new road, soon called the Mayberry Road, for one of the builders ended at Keen Camp, now called Mountain Center, where it joined other roads already in use. This made it easier to haul supplies and equipment to present day Garner Valley, where the dam was to be built.

Another problem facing Whittier and Mayberry, was how and where to obtain cement for the masonry work. Looking for what they considered the best cement available for the project proved to be a costly as well as a time consuming part of the operation. Finally, after many months, 11,000 barrels of Portland cement arrived in San Diego, California, shipped by boat from Brussels, Belgium. The barrels were then loaded on the train and hauled by rail to Hemet. Arriving there the cumbersome barrels were freighted up the mountain by mule-drawn wagons, over the recently completed Mayberry Road, the road built especially for the construction of the dam.

Fires were yet another problem. One fire destroyed the building housing the rock crusher causing a long delay while the building was being rebuilt and the rock crusher replaced. Weather proved to be another obstacle. Mother Nature did not always cooperate. Progress on the dam was held up or even set back several times because of flooding and water damage during heavy rainstorms.

Trees had to be cleared from the area where the future lake would be created. The downed trees were milled on site. This lumber was used in the construction of the flumes that would carry the water to the valley below, as well as being for the construction of warehouses, bunkhouses, and other needed buildings.

Cattle raised on the Arnaiz and Thomas ranches were a source of beef for the construction workers. Fruit and vegetables grown by the Arnaiz family were also a big part of the workers diet. Many of the more than one hundred workers spoke a language other than English and Spanish. According to old-timers Manuel Arnaiz, not only supplied much of the food for the workforce, but his fluency in several different languages made him valuable as an interpreter.

For many years, the fenced and guarded lake was not available for recreational use by the general public. It was not until the early 1930s that the restrictions were relaxed and fishing was finally allowed. Swimming is still not permitted, but many acres of improved day, or overnight campsites are found along the northern shore of the lake. In good weather many fishing boats can usually see out on the water. Lake Hemet has become one of the preferred camping and fishing spots for people throughout the mountain area.

When construction of the dam was completed in 1895, water had already been flowing down the flumes into the San Jacinto Valley for some time. The happy farmers around Hemet were by that time raising irrigated crops with the water collected in the mountain reservoir. With enough water the new town of Hemet flourished, just as Whittier and Mayberry had dreamed.

We will either find a way or make one-Hannibal
247-183 B.C.

No. ....

Notice of Location

Placer Claim

Claimant

J. F. Wellman

F. J. Hamilton

.... **Mining District**

.... **County** ....

DATED *July 6* / 19___

Walter D. Clark, Prompt Printer, Riverside Cal.

The Notice of Location for the Hamilton and Wellman placer mine in Kenworthy. Many of the local people did a little prospecting in the hills and canyons around Garner Valley and Anza besides their usual work.

Notice of Location - Placer Claim

Notice Is Hereby Given: That the undersigned citizens of the United States, over the age of twenty-one years, in compliance with the requirements of Chapter VI, Title 32, of the Revised Statutes of the United States and the local customs, laws and regulations, have this day located and claim the following described Placer Mining Grounds, to:

Lying ten rods south and 40 rods east from this monument located in sec 35 T 6 S, R. 4 E S.B.B.M

and have posted upon the discovery monument a duplicate of this said notice and that all minerals, and all veins, ledges, lodes or deposits within the lines of this claim, together with all water and timber appurtenant, allowed by law, are hereby claimed.

THIS CLAIM shall be known as the *Bear Pen*

_____ Placer Mining Claim

Said claim is situated in the *Kenworthy* _____ Mining District.

County of *Riverside* State of *Calif*

Section *35* Township *6* Range *4* Meridian *San Bern*

Located this *6* day of *July* 19 *31* This discovery

is made and the notice is posted this _____ day of *July* 19 *31*

Locators

J. F. Wellman
L. G. Hamilton

In July of 1931 Jim Wellman and his brother, Lincoln Hamilton, filed on a placer mine in section 35 of the Kenworthy mining District. The mine was called the Bear Pen Mine.

Chapter

6 Mining

Many of the early hill country people and sometimes others tried their luck at mining. Miners seeking the illusive gold and other minerals hidden in the rocky hills were some of the first to come into the mountains. There are old mine shafts and other signs of these early prospectors. The hill regions around both Anza and Garner Valley were the sites of numerous mining claims, but the hills and canyons to the east of Garner Valley were especially busy places for mining.

One of those early prospectors looking for gold above Garner Valley was Jesus Contreras. It was said that he had been more successful in finding gold than most. Contreras left the mountains and went back to Colton intending to return soon to recover what was said to be a quite large stash of gold that he had buried for safekeeping before he left.

For unknown reasons it wasn't until several years later when Contreras finally did return, accompanied by his grandsons. They were unable to find any sign of the buried gold. All that is left to show where the Contreras mine might have been are some concrete and stones, a part of what was once the arasta where the

31

unfortunate miner had ground ore while extracting his gold.

At one time there was even a thriving mining town in Garner Valley called Kenworthy. People have often wondered, was Kenworthy really a town or was it, as some say, just another mining camp that had failed? Mining camp or town, it was for a very short time, a bustling settlement with more than a hundred people living, mining, and working there.

Kenworthy was situated about a mile southeast of the present Kenworthy Ranger Station, and a little to the north of the Pathfinder Ranch. The one and only reason that Kenworthy existed was gold, gold that was never found in quantities that would make the mines a profitable operation.

In the eighteen hundreds there were many gold mines in the nearby hills. The old timers used to say that more money was probably made in the buying and selling of the mines, than there had ever been made from any gold taken from those mines.

The stories were that the mines were sometimes actually salted, making it easier to sell the poorly producing, or even worthless operations, to a gullible buyer. To salt a mine gold dust was loaded into a shotgun and then shot into the rocks. That was to make it look like there was actually enough gold to make it a profitable mine.

Mine salting probably had a lot to do with the situation when a wealthy and trusting English couple, Cara and Harold Kenworthy, became the main stockholders in the

Corona Mining and Milling Company. They had paid several thousand dollars to become the controlling owners of the company, a company that had been in operation for quite some time in the hills on the eastern side of the valley.

Soon after buying into the company around 1896, Harold Kenworthy, with his seemingly endless supply of money, spent thousands more when he began buying all sorts of expensive mining equipment. He then had the equipment shipped up the mountain to Kenworthy, the name he had given his new and fast growing settlement. Only the latest and best of equipment was bought and was set up ready for the recovery of the gold that he so eagerly looking forward to mining.

Many wagons loaded with lumber were hauled to the mining camp to be used in the construction of every kind of building ever found in a well-equipped mining operation. There were soon blacksmith shops, storerooms, a powder magazine, a barn, stables, a bunkhouses, a cookhouse, any kind of building that would be useful in a mining community was built. Mr. Kenworthy even built a fully operational assay office with a storage room to take care of the large quantities of gold that he anticipated finding.

Kenworthy School, which was soon ready for the younger residents of the community, had a longer life than did the town of Kenworthy. Kenworthy School was still in use in the early nineteen hundreds and had an important part in the education of the offspring of Thomas, Arnaiz, Scherman, Wellman, and Hamilton families, as well the children of any other nearby families.

33

Soon after the Kenworthys arrival the mining camp was boasting of an impressive two-story structure, the Corona Hotel, ready, it was said, to comfortably accommodate sixty or more guests. Besides the hotel and the bunkhouses, there were numerous cabins for the families of the many workers and miners, as well as a sizable home for the Kenworthys.

Nearby a large warehouse like structure was erected, the Lockwood General Merchandise Store operated by Charles W. and Emma Lockwood. Here the Lockwood store sold flour, bacon, and other necessary supplies. Charles Lockwood was also the postmaster for the newly opened Kenworthy Post Office, where residents and visitors could conveniently get their mail.

By 1898 Harold Kenworthy finally began to see that the mines were a losing proposition. He decided to sell his shares in the Corona Mining and Milling Company. Remember these were shares that the Kenworthys had originally paid thousands of dollars for, and in addition had spent thousands more on buildings and equipment. In the end Harold Kenworthy sold the Corona Mining and Milling Company for about ten dollars and moved on.

It was noted by the newspapers of the time that when the Kenworthys gave up and departed, one of the things left behind was the fully equipped assay office and storage room that had never been used.

The once booming town of Kenworthy did not have the distinction of becoming a real ghost town. In a very few years it just sort of disappeared.   The buildings were torn down and hauled away to other parts of the mountain and used in new buildings. The equipment was sold, stolen, or borrowed, vanishing just as the buildings had done. Soon little or nothing was left to show where the all but forgotten mining camp, built by a wealthy, but easy to fleece Englishman, had for a few short years been a bustling gold town called Kenworthy.

Workers at the Kenworthy mines and residents in Garner Valley got their groceries and mail at the C.W. Lockwood store in the 1890s. It was only in business for a short time during the boom times in the mining town of Kenworthy.

Chapter

7

HOMESTEAD ERA

Homesteading was not an easy life. To clear the redshank and sagebrush from the land and to build a livable house with only hand tools and no modern machinery took months and even years of hard labor. That was more than some of the homestead people could stand. Many left. Water was also a deciding factor in whether or not the venture would be a success. Roads names in Anza are like a roll call of early valley residents who did stay and build homes. Bohlen, Bahrman, Cary, Contreras, Kirby, Terwilliger, Tripp, and Wellman Roads all remind us of the pioneer families who stayed long enough to have a road named for them.

The government again made property on the Cahuilla Plains available for homesteading in 1909. Among the first to file on claims were some of the descendants of earlier settlers. John and Fanny Arnaiz Contreras filed on 160 acres of homestead land in Anza. Fanny was the daughter of Manuel and Dolores Arnaiz, earlier homesteaders in Garner Valley.

The Contreras homestead was located west of what is now Contreras Road and south of Johnson Road. Fanny tells how when she and her husband moved to the valley in 1910 and started clearing the brush from their land their only neighbor was *"one lonely bachelor, Henry Hamilton."* Henry was the son of early settler James Hamilton. Henry's homestead was the property where Ciro's Restaurant is now located.

Soon the brother and sister of Fanny and John Contreras, Antone and Daisy Arnaiz Contreras also filed on homestead land in Anza. Their property was the 160 acres to the east of Contreras Road adjoining the property of Fanny and John. The Contreras brothers were the grandsons of Jesus Contreras, the gold miner in the middle 1800s who couldn't find his buried gold in the hills above Garner Valley when he returned to the mountains years later.

Both couples spent long days clearing the sagebrush and redshank from their property to get the land ready to plant crops. Homesteading was not new to Fanny and Daisy Contreras since they had both helped with all the chores needing to be done on a nineteenth century homestead as they were growing up in Garner Valley.

Contreras Road is named for these early homestead people. Fanny and John Contreras never had children of their own but helped to raise several nieces and nephews. Daisy and Antone Contreras were parents of one son, Clarence who was a mountain resident most of his life.

In 1910 Joseph G. Scherman, a descendant of the Antone Scherman family, early logging people around Idyllwild, and his wife, Sophia, filed on a homestead claim in the Anza Valley. Joe G. Scherman was also one of the first forest ranger in the San Jacinto mountain area. The Scherman property in Anza was just to the east of Hill Street south of Highway 371.

There they dry farmed and raised a few cattle and a large family. Among the children in the Scherman family were Minta, Anna, Adolph, Joseph A., Katherine, Rhinehart, and Vincent. One child, a small boy, was accidentally shot and killed. His grave with a wooden cross was at the southern end of the Scherman property. For many years a white picket fence surrounded the grave. All traces of the fence and the marker are now gone.

Since there was no school building in Anza at that time, for a year or so, until Hamilton School was built in 1914, the Scherman's new barn was used as a classroom. A wooden floor and a heating stove had been added and Miss Eula DeVana began teaching the Scherman children and others from the surrounding area until the new Hamilton School was completed.

About four miles up Morris Ranch Road above Garner Valley, at what is now called Trails End, is a camp that was named for one of Joe G. Scherman's sons. In Orange County, that son, Joe A. Scherman, had become widely known as a capable U. S. Forest ranger interested in the preservation of our natural resources and also very active in youth groups. In his work he had heard that the Santiago Girl Scout Council of Orange County was looking for property for another camp.

Joe had also heard that his old classmate from school days at the Kenworthy School, and a lifelong friend, was selling his mountain property. It was through Joe's effort that a deal was made and Jim Wellman's 101 Ranch was bought for a Girl Scout camp and that it is now known as Camp Joe Scherman. The old ranch house on the property, now called the Wellman Museum, houses the extensive collection of Wellman Indian artifacts and big game specimens.

In about 1915 Noah and Alice Cary became homesteaders on the western side of the Anza valley near Cahuilla Mountain. After clearing out the sagebrush and redshank and fencing their property the family was ready to do some dry farming. Soon they had a large garden and had planted a few fruit trees.

Two of the Cary children, Art and Rose, attended Hamilton School as students. An older sister, May, taught at Hamilton School for a short time. Two other children, already grown, were Roe and Emily. Several of their grown children also filed and proved up on homestead claims of their own near the parents' homestead.

Several of the original Cary homestead structures are still standing and are presently in use by descendants of Noah and Alice Cary. A short section of Tripp Flats Road starting from Highway 371 has become known as Cary Road.

Son, Art Cary and his wife, Violet, continued to live on the old Clark ranch in Terwilliger up until the time of their deaths in recent years. They had purchased the ranch from Fred Clark in the late 30s. It was there that the Carys raised their two sons, Dick and Bob.

Another road named for a homestead family is Kirby Road. The Kirbys, Will and Mary also came to the valley in about 1915. Their children, Nellie and Jay, received a part of their education at the one room Hamilton School. The

Kirby property was due north of the Anza Electric Cooperative, just below what is now Mitchell Road. Besides dry farming the Kirbys were in the well-drilling business and dug many of the wells in the valley.

In 1916 Alma and Carl Bahrman chose property at the southern end of Terwilliger Valley on which to file a homestead claim. As with many of the homestead families, Carl Bahrman, continued to work in the city as a carpenter, earning money to support the rest of the family. Mrs. Bahrman and five of their children lived fulltime on the homestead while they cleared the land, built a home, and planted trees and crops in order to fulfill the requirements for proving up on homestead property.

Milton one of the younger Bahrman sons attended Hamilton School. In time Milton and an older brother, Lincoln, had a ranch of their own on Mitchell Road between Bautista and Bahrman Roads. Bahrman Road is named for this homestead family

Descendants of Alma and Carl Bahrman continue to live on the old homestead property in Terwilliger Valley. On the property is one of the county's better-kept family graveyards. The fenced and beautifully landscaped cemetery is the final resting place of the original homesteaders, Carl and Alma Bahrman, as well as a memorial to many other Bahrman descendants and relatives.

In 1919 Ray and Maude Fobes bought property above Garner Valley in the canyon that is now called Fobes Canyon. Ray Fobes had been a stage driver for many years making daily trips up and down the mountain between Hemet and Idyllwild with his team of white horses. Life for the couple changed completely when they bought their mountain property and turned it into a ranch that was known for its excellent produce, especially pears and cabbage.

Around 1945 Ray and Maude Fobes sold the property. By the late sixties there had been several different owners with many changes. For a time it was a commune owned by the LSD guru, Timothy Leary.

Over the years fires, neglect, and time have done their share in erasing almost all remnants of the original Fobes ranch. The trees were not cared for as carefully. Gardens were not planted. It is no longer a place noted for its fine produce. The barns and the house are gone and there is no mountain stream flowing between the house and the barns. About all that is left to remind one of the well-kept Fobes property are a few fruit trees, some still bearing those delicious pears that the ranch was noted for.

Around 1919 Jim and Elma Hall Wellman filed on their homestead claim. He was the son of Frank and Clara Arnaiz Wellman and the grandson of Manuel and Dolores Arnaiz, early mountain settlers. She was the brother of Dan Hall an earlier homesteader whose property was about where the Baptist church now stands. Elma and her younger brother, Harry, completed their elementary education at the original Hamilton School.

The Wellmans built a small house and made other improvements to prove up on their property at the northeast end of Anza Valley near where the James Hamilton home had stood in

41

earlier times. All that is left of the Wellman homestead is an old rock and concrete fireplace, still standing where the house burned to the ground nearly eighty years ago.

Jim Wellman was known throughout the mountain area as being a successful cattleman, hunter, trapper, big game guide, and tracker. His start in the cattle business was said to have begun at the age of nine with one bull calf. He earned the calf by irrigating a pasture for a San Jacinto rancher. The only way to get the calf home in the mountains was to lead the animal on foot up the old Keen Camp Grade. Walking, pulling the reluctant animal behind him on the end of a rope, nine-year old Jim finally, after many hours, reached home with the start of his cattle herd. Jim continued in the cattle business on his 101 ranch up until the time of his death.

Jim also had an early start hunting and trapping. In a 1914 issue of the Hemet News an item describes how at the age of thirteen he had trapped a lion that had been killing many of the family's livestock. Living so close to nature Jim became an expert in tracking animals. He put this talent to use as an official tracker for Riverside County taking part in many successful rescues of lost children and adults.

From 1931 to 1939 Jim Wellman was justice of the peace for Bergman Township, that is the Anza and Aguanga area. During his time as justice of the peace the living room of the Wellman home was frequently a courtroom, the scene of numerous trials. Fence disputes, illegal hunting, trespassing cattle, neighborhood feuds, and other legal matters all had their day in court.

Performing marriages was yet another duty performed by the justice of the peace. One marriage that he officiated at made a lasting impression on his family. At the bridal couple's request the Cahuilla people granted them permission to have their wedding rites conducted at the Cahuilla Cemetery on Ramona's grave. The pair arrived on a motorcycle for the ceremony, with both dressed entirely in black.

A more traditional wedding ceremony, also officiated by Jim Wellman was held at the home of Antone Contreras when he and Mrs. Evelyn Farrand were married. After that ceremony there was even the traditional and very noisy hill country chivaree. Neighbors came from miles around with noisemakers and food to launch the couple into their new life.

Henry Hamilton, son of early settler James Hamilton, was one of the lucky homesteaders with a good water supply. The Hamilton well on the south side of Highway 371 where Ciro's Restaurant is now located, produced more than enough water for his needs with water to spare. Many of the new settlers took advantage of his generosity and hauled water in drums by the wagonload from the Hamilton well. His willingness to share gave the newcomers time to solve their own water problems while getting started as homesteaders.

W.L. (Bill) Faust was a homesteader in the Terwilliger Valley arriving in around 1914. There on what is now Chapman Road between Bailey and Ramsey Roads, Bill built himself a little house and planted some apple, plum, and cherry trees. Some of Bill's grandchildren still live on a part of the original homestead and sadly remember one special apple tree that year after year produced many boxes of apples. The year their grandfather died the apple tree also died.

In a few short years Bill Faust had become the one carpenter most depended upon in the hill country for building. Among those buildings that he had built were the Litchwald store, Devaney's store, the R. L. Woods home in Durazno Valley, and the Jim Wellman and Lincoln Hamilton homes in Anza. His excellent workmanship, especially in the design and construction of very convenient kitchens, was well known. Anyone having a home built by Bill Faust appreciated the fine workmanship he had put into it.

The Bohlen place, now Minor property, is that property on the north side of Highway 371 between Kirby and Hill Street. When John Bohlen and his sisters arrived in Anza they were more fortunate than most people coming to start a homestead. They were able to purchase the Dick Shank property and to move into a comfortable house where there was plenty of water from an artesian well.

Most homesteaders in Anza had to think first of housing and water before anything else could be done. The Bohlens were able to get right to work with the business of farming. Their place soon had flower and vegetable gardens, and many kinds of fruit trees.

One of the sisters, Grace Bohlen, did file on and prove up on one hundred and sixty acres of homestead land. That property was up above Mitchell Road on Bohlen Road. The elementary school is on that piece of land. After Grace's death another sister, Nan, gave a part of the homestead property to the school district.

The Bohlen cement and rock reservoir stored water from the artesian well making it possible to do more irrigated farming than most farmers could do in the valley at that time. Their property was about the only one in the valley where alfalfa was raised before the deep irrigation wells were finally dug in the late 1940s.

John and Grace were the farmers in the family. Nan continued to work at a job in Los Angeles earning money for the family. Besides the trees and gardens the Bohlens also raised turkeys, guinea fowl, chicken, peacocks, and a few cattle, mostly dairy animals for milk and butter.

When the well's dry we know the worth of water,
Benjamin Franklin

Chapter

8

Cattle Ranching

For many years cattle ranching has been an important part of life in the San Jacinto Mountains. Even before the coming of the first settlers Indians were grazing cattle on the grassy meadows at Cahuilla. From the early 1800s or before large herds of cattle roamed the San Jacinto Valley and surrounding region on the huge Mexican land grants. During a severe drought in the San Jacinto Valley around 1864, the Estudillo cattle were dying of starvation. In order to save a part of their vast herds, some of the Estudillo cattle were driven into the mountains to graze in the lush mile high meadows around Idyllwild.

About that same time Charley Thomas, had heard about the superior grazing land in Garner Valley. Thomas was soon settled there with his cattle and racehorses. The family continued in the cattle business until 1907 when they sold out to R.F. Garner. Garner descendants still run cattle on part of what was the original Thomas ranch.

Frank Wellman, another early cattleman, ran cattle around Idyllwild and even farther up the steep mountainside above Idyllwild. Along Willow Creek the remains of a small log cabin are said to be those of a cabin built by this early cattleman. Moving into the vicinity of Anza, Aguanga, and Sage at about the same time with their large herds of cattle were the Reed, Parks, and Tripp families.

By the 1870s the James Hamilton family had arrived in Anza with their cattle and soon became a significant part of the cattle industry. Hamilton cattle spread out over the eastern part of the Cahuilla Plains, soon to be known as Hamilton Plains, up around Hog Lake on the side of Thomas Mountains, down into Coyote Canyon, and over into Garner Valley. They also ran cattle with the Arnaiz and Wellman livestock over the mountain on the desert side into Palm Canyon and beyond.

Coming in the 1890s were two more cattle ranchers, the Clark brothers, Fred and Frank. They settled in the Terwilliger and Durazno Valley areas south of Anza and continued ranching up into the 1930s. Coyote Canyon and below were usually places to find the Clark cattle. Clark Lake, Clark Well, and Clark Valley are all named for the Clarks.

Other ranchers' cattle could also be found grazing down in Coyote Canyon and the Borrego country during the winter. Cattle camps were established there in order to be near the cattle. In addition to the sites named for the Clarks, Joel Reed Valley and Parks Canyon were named for other early mountain cattlemen.

The Arnaiz family arrived in 1893 and their ranch was soon one of the largest in the area with cattle grazing throughout the southern end of Garner Valley, into the nearby canyons, and over the mountain into the area around Palm Canyon. Indian cowboys were employed to help the family

47

with the cattle.

Throughout the whole of the growing Arnaiz grazing territory cow camps were established at convenient places. Soon that territory took in much of the land on the desert side of the mountain, east to Palm Canyon, the Pinyon Flats, and around Asbestos Mountain. Sometimes the cattle were driven across Deep Canyon and into the Martinez and the Horse Thief country, grazing even as far down as desert floor.

Besides the cattle consumed by the Arnaiz family, many of their animals were butchered and the meat sold locally. Beef grown by the Arnaiz family also became a big part of the meat eaten by workers at the Kenworthy gold mines as well as for the workers building the Lake Hemet Dam. Large herds of Arnaiz cattle were driven down the mountain to the railroad in San Jacinto to be shipped to market.

Over the years, a number of the Arnaiz cattle were missed in the roundup in the backcountry. These missed animals became wild, what are called bronco cattle. One of those long horned bronco steers had shrewdly outwitted anyone attempting to catch him until he was finally roped in the late 1930s. When taken back to the ranch he would have nothing to do with human beings and refused to eat. Later when his carcass was skinned out it became evident why he had such an aversion for the human race. There were several lead bullets lodged in his carcass.

The cattlemen coming into the mountains weren't the only ones to be in the cattle business. Cahuilla Indians were already grazing their livestock on the lush meadows at Cahuilla and had probably been doing so since the time of the Mexican land grants, or before. The Indians have always been an important element in the mountain cattle business. Some raised their own cattle. Some leased their land to other cattlemen for pastureland. Still others worked on the nearby ranches as ranch hands and expert cowboys, many noted for their ability with a rope. Old-timers used to speak highly of the ability and reliability of the early Indian cattle people often mentioning members of the Costo, Alaveras, Lugo, Cassero, Guanche, Tortes, and Lubo families as well as others.

It wasn't until the late thirties that improved roads and trucks made it possible to move cattle in any way except to drive them. In the early part of the 1900s the Domenigoni family from the Winchester area would drive several hundred cows through the streets of Hemet to summer pasture in Idyllwild. In the earlier years traffic and fast cars weren't too much of a problem. Most people were very cooperative. Either they stopped their vehicle, and waited for the cattle to move on, or they drove slowly through the bunch. Even after the roads were paved the cattle were sometimes driven down the highway. It's a good thing that at that time most people didn't drive more than 35 or 40 miles per hour.

By 1907 R.F. Garner purchased the Thomas ranch and had brought in more cattle and had bought more land. In the late 1920s the Hamilton-Wellman-Arnaiz family sold most of their Garner Valley property to the Garner ranch. This included nearly the entire valley south of

Fobes Road, except for the Thomas Mountain Village property, and the piece of property where the "Kenworthy" house sits, that's the red house with the windmill in front along Highway 74.

The offspring of the first cattlemen began their own cattle operations on both sides of the mountain. In the Anza area, by the thirties there were several new ranchers raising a few cattle, among the new ranchers were the Bahrmans, Charlie Johnson, and Art Cary

Branding time in cattle country was always an exciting time. Anyone with a rope and a horse was sure be there hoping for a chance to catch a calf for the branding iron. In spite of the smoke, smell of burning hair, and the dust stirred up by the horses and cattle, the fence was usually lined with local people as well as outsiders wanting to get in on a little of the excitement. It was not unusual to have fifty or more people from all over watching on branding day.

Part of the attraction was the impromptu rodeo that might come after all the calves were branded and earmarked. Then the fun began when there would be steer riding and if someone had a horse that would buck and there was a person daring enough to try to ride it, there might even be some bronco riding. From time to time one team of ropers would challenge another to prove which team was the fastest at heading and heeling a cow. Some of the most expert ropers and riders at these events were from the reservation.

Until roads were improved and there were trucks capable of hauling large loads of livestock the   mountain cattlemen continued to do most of their ranch work in much the same way as it was done by those first cattlemen in the 1800s. It was hard dirty work and meant many hours in the saddle to do a day's work.

Now there are gooseneck trailers and dependable trucks to get horses and riders from on end of the range to the other in a few minutes, or an hour instead of a day. There are branding chutes that make branding the biggest animal a much quicker, cleaner, and easier task. Long drives through heat and dust, behind a herd of bawling cattle, don't happen as often when there are large cattle trucks, equipped to move the cattle quickly over paved roads.

Many of the backcountry trails used today by hikers and others were actually made by the early ranchers as they moved their cattle from range to range Those using the trails seldom realize that hard working pioneers, the cattle ranchers tending their cattle, were the ones who have made it possible for them to enjoy their backcountry experience. Trails that were grubbed out by ranchers through dense brush, make it possible for many to visit and enjoy the backcountry wilderness they might otherwise be unable to reach

Deer and other wildlife native to the hill country, where water is often hard to find, all take advantage of the water that the cattlemen developed and made available for their cattle. The ranchers also helped to prevent forest fires. Where grazing cattle have kept the weeds and brush under control brush or forest fires aren't nearly as disastrous as where the vegetation has become very dense.

Windmills were depended upon by many of the hill country
ranchers to pump water for their cattle.

Branding Hamilton, Arnaiz, and Hamilton cattle. Cattle ranchers started coming into the Anza and Garner Valley areas in the middle 1800s. For many years the raising of cattle was the main occupation of the mountain people.

53

SOME OLD CATTLE BRANDS OF THE MOUNTAINS

Arnaiz Family	6 6 **Clara Hamilton**	-101 **Jim Wellman**

Quitman Reed   **Lincoln and Louise Hamilton**

Garner Ranch   7OL **Jim Wellman Family**   **Antonio Contreras**

2 8 **Lincoln Hamilton**   **Frank Wellman**   **Jim Hamilton**

Jim Wellman and Lincoln Hamilton   **Tripp Family**

Cattle brands as drawn in 1978 by Jim Wellman, grandson of Manuel Arnaiz, and son of Frank Wellman.

54

Form 656

UNITED STATES DEPARTMENT OF AGRICULTURE
FOREST SERVICE

GRAZING PERMIT.

No. 6   *April* 8th, 1907.
                                                    (Date.)

Mr. *Manuel Arnaiz*, of *Valle Vista Calif.*
    (Name.)   (Place of residence.)

having presented receipt No. 32/35 showing that the grazing fee amounting to the sum of ....
Thirty nine 60/100 dollars ($ *39,60*), has been paid, is hereby authorized to pasture
the following number and class of live stock :

.... *Eighty (80)* .... head of cattle
.... *Six (6)* .... head of horses
.... head of sheep

Branded or earmarked :

...., upon reserved public lands

within the .... *San Jacinto* .... Forest Reserve

from *April 1st* 190 *March 31st*, 1908 ;

Provided, That the animals shall not intrude upon any area upon which grazing is prohibited, nor upon
any portion of the forest reserve except the following described area :

Sec. 8 T 7 S R 4 E, E½ Sec. 3, T 6 S R 4 E, as in
Pinon flats. Constant Canyon, as far north
as Magnita flats and Willow springs one mile
north, of Van Summers.

This permit is issued on the conditions that said .... *Manuel Arnaiz*

has, by his application No. *6*, dated *February 20*, 190 7, agreed to comply fully
with all forest reserve rules and regulations now or hereafter adopted.

This privilege is extended with no obligation or agreement on the part of the Government to maintain
an exclusive possession upon any part of said reserve to any one person or firm, nor as to adjustment of any
conflict as to possession.

For a violation of any of the terms of the application on which it is based, or whenever any injury is
being done the reserve by reason of the presence of the animals therein, this permit will be canceled and the
animals will be removed from the reserve.

                                        R. Bell,
                                        Forest Supervisor.

The 1907 grazing permit issued to Manuel Arnaiz allowing him
graze cattle in the Pinyon Flats area.

Above branding Hamilton cattle at Kenworthy
in the open in the 1800s

Cattle corralled at the Wellman ranch in Anza
for branding in the squeeze chute. 1930s.

56

Chapter

9

Farming

Farming was an important part of all early hill country life, but more so in Anza than in Garner Valley. In Garner Valley with their good supply of water the Arnaiz family raised a garden and had quite a large orchard. A little hay and grain crops were also grown, but the grassy meadows found there supplied much of the feed needed.

The Thomas family at the northern end of the valley was also fortunate in having an excellent water supply and plentiful pastureland.

Another place that had more than the usual amount of water and grassland was the Cahuilla Indian Reservation. In the early days the many springs and streams there furnished plenty of water for household use and for the livestock. Some people even had adequate water for a few fruit trees and a garden.

The people on the reservation were also fortunate in having a hot spring that they kindly allowed others to use on laundry day. The warm sulphur water was the best for miles around in which to scrub clothes clean. For many years their swimming pool was also shared with others. In a community where there was no other body of water large enough to get wet in, their pool was a favorite gathering place.

Many of the homestead people did not have an adequate source of water and depended on a neighbor's generosity. Sometimes water was hauled for miles in a horse drawn wagon loaded with barrels of water for the homesteader's thirsty cattle. Others toted the water home, one pail in either hand, as they trudged home across the fields with the heavy buckets full of the water needed for household use.

In Anza there was rarely enough water in the amounts needed for irrigated crops. The Bohlen's artesian well furnished enough water to grow a small field of alfalfa and to irrigate several fruit trees and a good sized garden. But dry farming, which is the planting and growing of grain crops without the help of any irrigation, was the only way for most of the farmers to get a crop. A good harvest depended almost entirely on the weather and the amount of rain that came.

For many years farming in the hills continued to be done in this same way with little or no modern equipment. The field was prepared for planting with a horse-drawn plow. Then the seed was planted by hand or with a planter pulled behind a mule or horse.

After that the farmer waited and watched, hoping for the rain to come in the right amounts and at the right time. After waiting and watching the weather for weeks, or even months, the oats or other grain might or might not make a good crop, all depending on the weather. If there was a crop to be harvested it was done by hand or by horse-drawn machinery.

By the thirties farmers were using some motorized equipment, but many farmers still depended upon teams of horses or mules to pull the plows and harvesting machinery. During harvest the large crews would pull into a field and mow the field, rake the cut grain, and then either thresh the grain, or bale the hay. Finishing one field they moved on to the next doing the same in each field. Much of the harvesting was done cooperatively with the farmers getting together to make up the crews to man the harvesting machines.

The wife of the farmer whose field was being harvested that day usually served the harvesting crew a hot meal at noon. Getting a hardy meal ready for ten to fifteen hungry men was no easy chore in the days when there were none of the conveniences we now have. All the food was cooked from scratch without the help of freezers, modern stoves, electricity, or a local and well-stocked super market.

To prepare a hardy meal for the harvest crew usually called for long hours over a blazing wood burning cook stove in an overheated kitchen. Sometimes the women would help each other with the meals as the harvesting crew moved from field to field.

Water and its lack was always a major problem in the days before electricity and deep irrigation wells. A windmill pumping water from a shallow well did not produce water in the quantities needed for irrigated crops. At that time there was no way of getting the equipment necessary for digging deeper wells. That meant that until 1949 when the equipment was available to dig to a greater depth the raising of hay and grain crops were done only by dry farming.

In 1947 Lincoln Hamilton, a grandson of early settler James Hamilton, was finally successful in digging a deep irrigation well, a well that would completely change the way that agriculture in Anza. His deep wells produced enough water to irrigate many acres of commercial crops. Farmers no longer needed to rely entirely on the weather to cooperate, in order to get a good crop.

Over the next few years, using water from his deep wells, Lincoln Hamilton experimented with growing many different water thirsty crops, including alfalfa hay, alfalfa seed, potatoes, sugar beet seed, and gladiolas, all on a commercial basis. The most colorful years were those years when Lincoln raised gladiolas. Many people have described the valley at that time as looking like a rainbow. Several rows of bulbs all one color were planted, making a strip several yards wide. Many strips, all different colors planted side-by-side reminded one of a rainbow, when the flowers were in full bloom.

Soon other local farmers had dug deep irrigation wells and were harvesting their own irrigated crops. In recent years Agri Empire has done most of the farming in the valley, with potatoes as their main crop. Since Lincoln Hamilton dug that first deep well in 1947 the whole area has changed from a valley with family farms, where hay and grain crops were raised by dry farming, to an area that generally produces irrigated crops being raised by one farming group.

The Scherman barn where school was held
until the Hamilton School was built in 1914.

John and Fanny Arnaiz Contreras built this house in about 1925,
the first house in Anza to have an indoor bathroom with all
fixtures and running water.

61

The lack of water was always a problem in the early days. In the 1920s Jim Wellman and Lincoln Hamilton hauled this tank, balanced on the back of the truck, for almost one hundred miles. The last thirty miles were over rough mountain roads.

Dolores Garduna Arnaiz on left and some of her children and grandchildren

Until the first deep irrigation wells were dug in the late 1940s most all farming in the hill country was dry farming that is done without any irrigation.

Time for an outing.

The Devaneys and Clara Hamilton

63

Above The Litchwald store where the post office was when it first became Anza. Bertha Litchwald was the postmaster at that time. *Below* The Devaney store. The post office was in this building for over twenty years until Clark and Nell Devaney retired around 1958. Notice Hamilton School, built in 1914, in the background

Chapter

10 Mountain Post Offices

There have been post offices in many different areas in the mountain communities. Sometimes the post offices were nearby, other times the residents in an area had to travel many miles to pick up their mail, often as far away as Oakgrove, Sage, and Idyllwild. At times they even had to travel as far as Valle Vista and San Jacinto.

The post office in Anza was known by many different names. For many years it was Cahuilla. In about 1913 the post office was a corner in the Shaney home on what is now Mitchell Road, due north of the present Anza post office. There it was called Baptiste. By 1918 the post office had been moved again, this time to the Mead home on the north side of the road near the corner of Mitchell and Bahrman Roads. There it was the Bautista Post Office. In 1926 while the post office was in the Litchwald store Bertha Litchwald was postmaster and it became Anza. By 1935 it was in the Devaney store, but was still called Anza with Nell Devaney as postmaster.

Cahuilla was a post office name at various times and at different sites, including the reservation. According to an old article from a

1926 issue of the *Hemet News* the people at the Cahuilla Indian Reservation wanted the Cahuilla Post Office to be on the reservation, not in Anza. That news article reported, *"One of the main reasons for changing the name was the claim of the Indians at the Cahuilla reservation that they wanted a post office established there, with the name Cahuilla, while the post office which has borne that name for several years is located six miles from the reservation."*

When the people living in the eastern part of the valley found that they could no longer use the name Cahuilla for the post office they chose the name Hamilton. At that time the eastern part of the valley was usually called Hamilton Plains, or sometimes Bautista. The residents wanted to call their post office Hamilton in honor of the early settler, James Hamilton. But the name Hamilton was not available. There was already a city with the Hamilton name in the northern part of the California.

Bautista and Babtiste, both previous names for the local post office, were also choices, but they could no longer be used either. Those names had caused confusion with another post office with a similar name in the northern part of the state. Finally in 1926 the name Anza was decided upon, honoring Juan Bautista De Anza.

The Kenworthy post office was established in the late 1890s at the mining town of Kenworthy, the short-lived mining town started by Harold Kenworthy. The post office was in existence for only a few years when the town and the post office were abandoned. For many years after that the Garner Valley people could pick up their mail at the post office at Keen Camp. That post office was situated about where Living Free is now. Later the name Keen Camp was changed to Mountain Center and the post office was moved to its present location at Mountain Center.

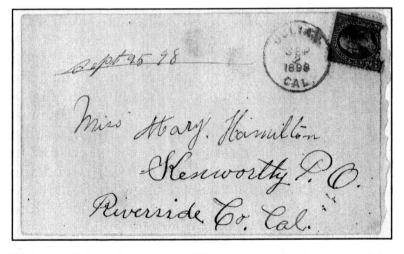

Mail was delivered to many different mountain locations with many different post office names. For a few years there was a post office in the town of Kenworthy, now called Garner Valley. The mining town, of about two hundred people, was situated about a mile south of the Kenworthy Ranger station and north of the Pathfinder Ranch.

Chapter

11   SCHOOLS

Quite a bit of creativity was used in the early days in getting the mountain children educated. Learning was done in homes, barns, a recycled hotel, and one-room schoolhouses. Since there was no bus, students got to school any way they could. At great many arrived at school on foot, riding a horse or burro, or in a buggy. In later years they might come to school in the family car if the roads were in good enough shape to be drivable. Roads were always a problem in wet weather.

Families lived miles apart making it difficult to have enough children in one place to have a school. Sometimes a family would hire a teacher and hold classes for their own children in their home. It was not unheard of for the children of another family to be taken into a home where a teacher had been hired and the children of both families being taught by one teacher. Sometimes the teacher rotated from house to house teaching different families.

One of the first schools in the hill country was the school built in the eighteen hundreds by Will and Shasta Tripp. Children from their two large families attended the little one room school near their homes at Tripp Flats for their elementary schooling

In the early 1890s before the Kenworthy School was built there was a small boarding school in Anza run by the Casner family. Clara Arnaiz used to tell how for a short time she and her older brother, Gene, had attended that school along with a few other students from both Garner Valley and Anza.

Another little one-room school was at the Kenworthy mining town in Garner Valley. That school had been built for the children of the workers during the boom time beginning around 1896. Later when the boom was over lumber from the abandoned Corona Hotel was recycled and made into another school. It came to be known as the Hamilton school since it was close to the Hamilton home. The Hamilton, Arnaiz, Wellman, Scherman, and other children living in the Garner Valley area attended that school.

The Hamilton School District in Anza was formed in 1913, but a school building for the new district hadn't been built yet. Classes were held for a year or so in Joe Scherman's new barn. A floor had been put down in one part of the barn. The Scherman children and a few others from the surrounding area did their learning there. Miss Eula DeVana was the teacher for all eight grades.

Finally, by the fall of 1914, the one room Hamilton School was finished and ready for students. George Turner had donated two of his 160 acres of land to the new Hamilton School District on which to build the school. His property was west of Contreras Road and south of Highway 371. That building has become a landmark in the valley.

The one room schoolhouse with the bell

tower on top was built by volunteer labor. Several valley men hauled the lumber up the mountain over the old unpaved Keen Camp Road in wagons pulled by teams of mules and horses from San Jacinto.

After hauling the lumber through Garner Valley they continued on into the Anza Valley over the steep dirt road, now called Hamilton Grade across the lower end of Thomas Mountain. Upon reaching Anza those men and others worked to erect the building and in time had it, according to old-timers, painted white and ready for the students to begin classes by the fall of 1914.

An October 1926 issue of the *Hemet News* reported, *"Tuesday was Clean-up Day at Hamilton School. A number of people of the community came in and put the yard and buildings in excellent condition."*

Up until the time that the Hamilton School District joined Hemet Unified School District community volunteers continued to show interest in the school by keeping the building, the schoolyard, and the windmill in good order. In the 1930s there was a need at school for a new shelter and place to keep feed for the student's horses. I can remember my father building a shelter with several stalls and a feed room so that we could tie our horses out of the weather while attending class.

The color of school changed over the years from white, to tan, to a light green depending on the color paint that was available. All who attended school there in the early days agree that the school was painted many different colors at different times, but that the color was never red. It has only been in recent times that it has been red and has become known as "The Little Red Schoolhouse."

A few other one-room schools were scattered throughout the mountain area, some in use for only for a short time. One of these schools was the Kenworthy Indian Emergency School. In the middle thirties many of the children from the Santa Rosa Reservation weren't able to attend school regularly because of the poor road conditions. Highway 74 had been paved but the road to Anza was still dirt. To make it possible for those children to attend school a little one-room school was built about a quarter of a mile north of what is now called Paradise Corners, at the junction of Highways 74 and 371. Several students came from Santa Rosa and five six of us living in Garner Valley also attended classes there.

Another small one room school in existence for only a few years was the Cahuilla School down near the Bergman Museum in Aguanga. The nearest school for those children had either been the Cottonwood School in Sage or Hamilton School in Anza. Because of the poor road conditions both those schools were at times impossible to reach in winter.

In the early years there were no buses. Burros or horses were the number one way of getting to school, but many students had no choice and walked, sometimes several miles to school. Children who lived far from school sometimes stayed with a family that lived closer to the school. Fanny and John Contreras often had someone else's child in their home so that

that child could attend school.

It is only in recent years that there has been any schooling beyond the elementary grades in the hill country. Many of the young people didn't get an education past eighth grade. Before the time of paved roads it was not unusual for a family to move away when their children reached high school age.

Students were fortunate if their family had relatives near a high school where they could stay and attend school. For others the only way to get more education was to find a family near a high school in need of some kind of help. Arrangements were made for the student to work for room and board. The work could be anything from housework or babysitting to feeding the pigs.

Since the roads were all dirt and unimproved, getting back up the hill on weekends could be a problem. Sometimes during wet weather the students were stranded in town for weeks at a time. After the roads were paved and a bus was used to haul students down the hill to high school it was still not easy to get an education. Taking the bus to high school meant a ride of many hours, leaving before sunup and getting home after dark.

Kenworthy School children on an outing. The little girl center front is Mary Wellman, daughter of Frank and Clara Arnaiz Wellman. In the 1890s there was a school in the town of Kenworthy. The Scherman, Arnaiz, Hamilton, and Wellman children attended school along with other children, many the offspring of the workers from the Kenworthy mines. After the town was abandoned parts of the Corona hotel were used to make another school, closer to the Hamilton home. It was sometimes called Hamilton School.

Chapter

12

Pines to Palms Highway

It is very easy to forget that it has not always been possible to reach the San Jacinto or Coachella Valleys from the mountains over paved roads in as little as forty-five minutes. Until the early nineteen thirties there was no road at all directly to the desert from the mountains.

Anyone wanting to go down that side of the mountain either walked or rode a horse using the trails that had been established by the Cahuilla Indians long ago. That route could mean a long hot hike or horseback ride over rough trails. The other choice would be to take the even longer route to the Coachella Valley over winding roads around by the San Jacinto Valley, Beaumont, Banning, and Palm Springs.

At that time travelers to the mountains from the San Jacinto Valley took the old Mayberry Road. Near Oak Cliff the road followed the left bank of the South Fork of the San Jacinto River. After driving through the water at Strawberry Creek, no bridge then, the old road continued on up Dry Creek Canyon with several switchbacks, ending near where McCall Park is now.

The Hemet Land and Water Company built the Mayberry Road in 1891 when the Lake Hemet Dam was under construction. The grade was so difficult that the passengers more often than not, had to get out and walk up the steepest grades in order to lighten the load. Sometimes they were even required to help push the vehicle as it struggled up the mountain.

Around 1926 Riverside County prisoners using hand tools, wheelbarrows, and horse drawn Fresno scrapers, began work to improve the Mayberry Road from Oak Cliff to Keen Camp. New sections of the road were constructed on the north side of the canyon a little higher than the old road.

At Dry Creek instead of following that canyon up the mountain, the new road turned west. The new part of the road climbed up the north side of the main canyon for a mile or so before turning back to the east. This made a much more gradual and easier climb to the mountains. Improvement of the road was finished around 1929 and became part of the present Highway 74.

For many years the road from Keen Camp down through Garner Valley and on to Vandeventer Flat at the Santa Rosa Indian Reservation was just a rough, unimproved wagon track. Soon after the beginning of improvements on the Mayberry Road, work also began on that stretch of road. One thing they didn't change at that time was the fine old pine tree that was left in the very middle of the highway a short distance north of Thomas Mountain Village. It stood there for many years in the middle of the paved highway, but was finally cut down for safety reasons.

Beginning around 1919 there was much discussion and debate about the best route for a road to the desert. Should it take the Rincon Trail from Santa Rosa to the desert floor, or was the

Dead Indian Canyon Trail better? Those in Palm Springs, in particular, wanted the route to go down the Rincon Trail, the old Indian trail that wound down Palm Canyon. Those to the east and south in the Coachella Valley favored the Dead Indian Canyon Trail and felt that it was better suited for a road. After much discussion the Dead Indian Canyon Trail was finally chosen.

Several voiced the opinion that it would not be possible to build a road down the Dead Indian Canyon route through solid rock and over such a steep mountainside. After months of hot, dirty work with picks, shovels, and horse drawn Fresno scrapers, and much blasting with dynamite, the county prisoners had worked their way down the mountain, making the numerous switchbacks that are still a part of a highway. Many considered that section of Highway 74 to be another wonder of the world. Riverside County prison labor had successfully constructed that section of road from just below Pinyon Flats to the desert floor.

The Federal Bureau of Public Roads constructed the middle section of the road between the forest boundary below Pinyon Flats and Santa Rosa. The completion of this part of the road in July 1932 made it possible to at last drive a vehicle up and down both sides of the mountain.

The highway was paved from the desert up over the mountain and down to the San Jacinto Valley by the mid nineteen thirties. Later, in 1971, State Highway 74, or the "Pines to Palms Highway" as it was called it, was named a scenic highway and is one of the longest scenic highways in Southern California.

Chapter

13
Camp Anza

There are many signs of the civilian army invasion that occurred in the San Jacinto Mountains starting in May of 1933. Some of these signs are an old log building, a public campground, and the rock shelter on the side of San Jacinto Peak, as well as many trails, firebreaks, and roads that are still in use. Young men who had enrolled in the Civilian Conservation Corp (CCC) made these signs of the past.

To combat some of the problems caused by the depression and the high unemployment rate among young men across the United States President Franklin Roosevelt had passed a bill setting up the CCC. The goal of the CCC was to conserve and develop our natural resources while giving employment and training to young men. About 250,000 men throughout the country took advantage of the program. In exchange for meals, uniforms, and a small monthly wage that went mostly to the dependent families of the men, these young men were put to work on worthwhile project that continue to be appreciated.

One interesting reminder of the CCC invasion is the wooden log building that was once a part of what was called Camp Anza in Burnt

Valley. For a short time Camp Anza was one of the most active and productive of the five CCC camps here on the mountain.

The Hemet News from that time glowingly praised the work of the CCC men and described how a small group from the camp was building a free campground in the Pinyon Flats area. The writer felt that the Pinyon Flats campground would be used and appreciated for years to come by the people who would be coming up from the desert heat to enjoy the cooler air.

Camp Anza was begun in June of 1933 and seemingly overnight became a bustling army post with 200 well-behaved young men from Youngstown, Ohio and another 10 army officers and California Division of Forestry personnel to oversee them. On August 4th of that year they had an impressive dedication and flag-raising ceremony, with the San Jacinto Lion's Club officiating. Noisy army planes from March Air Base circled overhead while a representative of the Anza Chamber of Commerce raised the United States flag above the camp.

By that time men from Camp Anza had already become known for expertly suppressing fires, as well as for the other improvements and construction they had done. September of that same year, men from the camp began working on the trail through Coyote Canyon. Beginning at the Fred Clark Ranch, they widened and improved the trail to Willow Springs, a distance of 12 miles. The reasoning for this was for better fire protection and for easier access by visitors to the area. Before that time the trail was only passable on foot or by horseback.

At the same time there was another CCC camp located at the Kenworthy Ranger Station in Garner Valley. CCC men at both camps worked hard five days a week, from seven in the morning until three in the afternoon. Baseball, boxing, books, newspapers, and radios all helped to occupy the men in their spare time. Sometimes there were dances held at Camp Anza with local people and others attending as guests. Trips off the hill were looked forward to.

Men from the CCC camps became a source of workers who had really learned to work. Some were hired locally for ranch work after they had finished their CCC enrollment and became permanent and productive residents of the state.

Grab a chance and you won't be sorry
for what might have been.
Unknown

Chapter

14

Helping Hands

Volunteering and helping each other was a way of life for many of the early people. The ranchers helped each other at roundup and branding time. Farmers worked together to get the crops harvested. When someone's home burned people from miles around came with clothing and food and helped to rebuild the home. In 1913 when a classroom was needed the Scherman family loaned their barn. In 1914 volunteers built the schoolhouse that has become a landmark in the community.

When the roads were just dirt tracks many people did their share of keeping the rocks out of the roadway and filling in the potholes. It was not unusual for the passengers to get out of the wagon and walk to ease the load the horses had to pull up the hill. As the passengers walked they helped to keep the roadway in a better condition by tossing rocks to the side.

The building of the Terwilliger hall and the Anza Community Hall are other examples of what volunteers have done in the hill country. In the late 1940s people saw that there was a need for a community hall. Until then most community events including dances, church services, voting, and public meeting had been held in the old Hamilton School. Lincoln Hamilton's cement floored equipment barn had become a favorite for dances by the 1940s, but everyone could see that it was really needed more to store machinery than to be used for dances.

All agreed that the only way to get a hall was to raise the money and to build it. The thing that almost split the community apart was in deciding where the hall should be built. One group wanted it in Terwilliger; another said that the eastern part of the valley would be a better place. Still another group was certain that the only logical place would be on the western end of the valley.

The Terwilliger group withdrew from the debate and proceeded to build a hall where they wanted it to be on Bailey Road in Terwilliger. That hall has served the entire valley well ever since. It was in use by the early 1950s even before the Anza hall was completed.

The problem of deciding on a suitable site for the Anza hall was finally settled when the Litchwald family offered to give the community the property on which to build the hall. Since it was centrally located, near the grocery store, and on the main road it was agreed upon by most to build on the Litchwald property. The only stipulation connected with the gift was that no liquor ever be served on the property. That requirement wasn't put in writing and it was soon forgotten.

Even after the disagreement over where to put the hall was settled there was further debate. This time it was over the size of the proposed Anza hall. One group felt that the size of the planned building was way too big for the number of people living in Anza at that time. The other group felt that the building should be much larger even than the size that was finally decided upon and built.

The building of both halls was financed and built by the local people. Bake sales, raffles, dinners, and bazaars were all a part of the community efforts to raise money for the construction projects. Recycled materials were used when possible, especially in the Anza hall. Volunteers took their trucks to March Air Base and returned loaded down with much of the discarded building material that went into the construction of the hall.

Valley residents, friends, and families, did most of the actual construction. Many weekends were spent helping to erect the new building. Ladies vied with each other in trying to serve the workers the best and the most. Money raising events continued throughout the entire time of construction and beyond. By 1952 the Anza Community Hall was also finished and ready for use.

Fire protection in the mountain areas is another area that was largely done by volunteers, except for the crew Kenworthy ranger station in Garner Valley. It had been there for many years. For several years beginning in 1933 the CCC men gave even more fire protection to the mountain areas. Beginning in the late thirties a small crew of fire fighters was stationed in Anza.

In 1959 the Cahuilla Volunteer Fire Service was formed with less than twenty members and an old pickup truck that was used to get the firemen to a fire. For many years the volunteer firemen organized and put on the very successful annual 4th of July parade.

Volunteer fire protection was a little slower in coming to Garner Valley. The Kenworthy ranger station with its small crew had been there for years but it wasn't until much later that a volunteer group was formed. Probably one reason that volunteer protection was so slow in coming to that area was because the southern end of the valley was very sparsely populated until it was subdivided. After it was subdivided in the middle 1970s Jack Garner donated land at the corner of Morris Ranch Road and Highway 74 for a firehouse. Volunteer labor built the fire station and volunteers for many years then manned it.

There are other groups, too numerous to mention that have been very active in serving the mountain communities, but there is one that has been in existence longer than most. The Anza Thimble Club was started in about 1912 and has been contributing to the community ever since in many ways. Bazaars, raffles, bake sales, and dinners all help to raise money that is then donated to the volunteer firemen, the schools and other worthy organizations. The Thimble Club started with just a few of the homesteaders and has been sewing and giving ever since.

Looking back at the history of Garner Valley and Anza there have been many changes in place names, the way of life, and the people who have lived here, but one thing that hasn't changed is the willingness of many of the people to help each other.

The Cahuilla people shared their food with

other native groups in time of need. The ranchers and farmers in Garner Valley and Anza helped each other. When a school was needed volunteers built one. Even today volunteers continue to lend a hand where they can to help keep the mountain area a preferred place to live for many.

One of the most active clubs in the hill country has been the Thimble Club, started in 1912. Bazaars, dinners, bazaars and other money raising projects have provided the money to pay for everything from scholarships for students to a resuscitator for the Cahuilla Volunteer Fire Service, the first volunteer firemen in the valley.

Appendix

Resources

Books of interest on mountain and local history including several on the Cahuilla people

Barrows-Ethno-Botany of the Cahuilla Indians
Bean-The Cahuilla Indians of Southern California
Bean-Temalpakh, Cahuilla Knowledge and Usage of Plants
Brigandi-Temecula, at the Crossroads of History
Elliott-History of San Bernardino and San Diego Counties
Frederick-Legends and History of the San Jacinto Mountains
Gabbert-History of Riverside County
Gardiner-The Hyatt Legacy
Gunther-Riverside County, California Place Names
Hemet/San Jacinto Genealogical Society-San Jacinto Valley Past and Present
Lawson-History of Lake Riverside
Holmes-History of Riverside County, California
Hubbard-Favorite Trails of the Desert Riders
Jackson-Ramona
James-The Cahuilla Indians
Jaenke -In the Olden Days
Lawton-Willie Boy
Maxwell-The E-Max Almanac
Maxwell-Pictorial History of the San Jacinto Mountains
Parker-The Historic Valley of Temecula
Reed-Old Time Cattlemen and Other Pioneers of the Anza Borrego Area
Reed-Old Timers of Southeastern California
Robinson-The San Bernardinos
Robinson-The San Jacintos
Robinson-The Story of Riverside County
Saubel-I'Isniyatam, (designs) A Cahuilla Word Book
Shipek-The Autobiography of Delphina Cuero
Smith-Indian Picture Writing of San Bernardino and Riverside Counties
Smith-Juan Antonio, Cahuilla Indian Chief, a Friend of the Whites
Tapper-The Friendliest Valley

Additional publications of interest

High Country is a quarterly magazine that was published years ago in Temecula. It has a great many stories of local interest, but is now out of print and hard to find. Many libraries have copies for reference use only.

Desert Magazine, another out of print publication that carried many articles of local interest.

The old issues of the *Hemet News* and the *Riverside Press Enterprise* have a wealth of information and both newspapers are on microfilm at some of the libraries.

Web sites for those interested in Juan Bautista De Anza include diaries, maps, lesson plans, and other information on the Anza expeditions.

http://anza.uorgon.edu/
http://www.desertusa.com

Index